Adult ADHD Relationships

A Partner's Guide to Understanding and Connection

Sam Goddiss

Copyright © 2024 by Sam Goddiss

All rights reserved.

No portion of this book may be reproduced in any form without written permission from the publisher or author, except as permitted by U.S. copyright law.

This publication is designed to provide accurate and authoritative information in regard to the subject matter covered. It is sold with the understanding that neither the author nor the publisher is engaged in rendering legal, investment, accounting or other professional services. While the publisher and author have used their best efforts in preparing this book, they make no representations or warranties with respect to the accuracy or completeness of the contents of this book and specifically disclaim any implied warranties of merchantability or fitness for a particular purpose. No warranty may be created or extended by sales representatives or written sales materials. The advice and strategies contained herein may not be suitable for your situation. You should consult with a professional when appropriate. Neither the publisher nor the author shall be liable for any loss or damages, including but not limited to special, incidental, consequential, personal, or other damages.

First edition 2024

Contents

Introduction		1
1.	What is Adult ADHD?	5
	Common Symptoms and Challenges	
	Types of ADHD	
2.	Myths & Misconceptions	16
	Myth #1: ADHD Isn't Real	
	Myth #2: People With ADHD Just Need To Try Harder	
	Myth #3: Only Boys/Men Have ADHD	
	Myth #4: People With ADHD Can't Focus—Ever	
	Myth #5: Only Children Have ADHD	
	Myth #6: ADHD Is The Same For Everyone	
	Recognizing the Realities of ADHD	
3.	The Impact on Relationships	24
	ADHD and Communication	
	Emotional Regulation and Impulsivity	
	Intimacy and Connection	
	The Inevitability of Anger	
4.	Empathy and Compassion	47
	Developing Empathy for Your Partner with ADHD	
	Practicing Patience	

Building a Supportive Environment

5. Strategies for Effective Communication 56
    Communication Difficulties Caused By Adult ADHD
    Developing Strategies for Effective Communication

6. Setting Realistic Expectations 65
    Managing Expectations in the Relationship
    Balancing Responsibilities
    Goal Setting and Accomplishments

7. Seeking Professional Help 69
    The Importance of Diagnosis
    Therapy and Counseling Options
    Medication and Treatment
    The Role of Support Groups

8. Self Care for Partners 77
    Taking Care of Your Mental Health
    Finding Balance in the Relationship
    Avoiding Burnout

9. Strengthening the Bond 83
    Nurturing Emotional Intimacy
    Activities and Strategies to Connect

10. The Road Ahead 88
    Celebrating Progress
    Continuing to Learn and Adapt
    Sustaining a Loving Relationship

11. Embracing Love and Growth 92

12. References 94

About the Author 100

Introduction

In the intricate dance of love, there exists a unique choreography. It's a dance where understanding waltzes with complexity, and where empathy intertwines with challenges.

This can be especially true for those in relationships where one partner (or both) have ADHD.

If you've got this book in your hands, chances are you've already taken a few spins on this dance floor, and you know it's not always a smooth waltz. It's more like a tango with moments of brilliance and frustration, a cha-cha of love and patience, and sometimes, a solo act of sheer resilience.

I want to start this by saying I'm not a doctor. This isn't the culmination of decades of research on ADHD, or relationships, or mental health. Instead, it emanates from the perspective of understanding, a decade-and-a-half-long journey lived, learned, and shared.

I've walked in your shoes, navigating the intricacies of love alongside someone whose world is colored by ADHD.

He takes a thousand years to read a short paragraph. If I send multiple texts throughout the day, when he finally checks them, he answers one. Just one. And usually it's the last one sent.

He asks me a question I just answered 2.5 seconds ago because what I said went in one ear and right out the other. Sound familiar?

When my (now) husband and I first moved in together, we'd been dating for years—some long distance. I had grown used to some of his idiosyncrasies. Cohabitating brought a new perspective not only to our relationship, but to the way ADHD impacted that relationship.

I was stuck. I wanted to fix it—fix him—and the problems it was causing in our relationship.

I know now that this wasn't the right way to look at things. There is no fixing him because there's nothing *wrong* with him.

But, at the time, I was looking for answers.

There are so many books out there about loving a child with ADHD. About parenting and helping a child cope. But not nearly enough about how adults with ADHD struggle, especially the unique struggles and triumphs of adults with ADHD within the realm of love and relationships.

I did the research. I tried to understand. Too often, I found myself flipping through the pages of irrelevant books, seeking answers that eluded me. I had to cobble together half answers and try to figure out what was relevant and what wasn't.

It was frustrating and time consuming and it left me without a lot of the answers I'd been searching for.

INTRODUCTION

This is the book I wish I'd been able to find.

Millions of adults are impacted by ADHD. Diagnosed or not, ADHD is an invisible thread that weaves through the fabric of countless partnerships, sometimes unnoticed but often deeply felt.

ADHD can strain even the most resilient of bonds. It can be the invisible hand that pushes love away, causing confusion, hurt, and doubt. But it doesn't have to be this way.

Truly understanding your partner and their struggles can go a long way in improving your relationship.

With knowledge as your compass and empathy as your guide, you have the power to navigate the challenges and cultivate a love that transcends ADHD's complexities.

Remember that you are not alone.

I wrote this book to help those who are in the same position I found myself in fifteen years ago. My goal is not only to enrich your understanding of your partner and their ADHD, but also empower you to build stronger, healthier, and more loving relationships through understanding and compromise.

One of the most important things to remember, I've found, is that much of this is out of their control. They're not trying to hurt you or ignore you. They're not being lazy or procrastinating.

Their brains simply work differently.

And the more we understand that, the more we accept it and work with our partner—instead of trying to fix them for our own benefit—the better the outcome.

Chapter One

What is Adult ADHD?

Let's begin by unraveling the acronym. As you know, ADHD stands for attention deficit hyperactivity disorder. Unsurprisingly, it can impact a person's ability to pay attention, thus "attention deficit." It can also cause individuals to carry excess energy that can be disruptive; this is the "hyperactivity."

But that's hardly all ADHD is.

It is a neurodevelopmental disorder, which is a fancy way of saying ADHD brains are different in their structure and operation.

ADHD is not a sign of low intelligence or laziness.

It is a recognized condition that affects how someone processes information, regulates emotions, and organizes behavior. This can spill over into various aspects of life, such as work, school, relationships, and even self-esteem.

While ADHD begins in childhood, it doesn't simply disappear when the clock strikes midnight on their 18th birthday. It can—and often does—persist into adulthood. In the United States alone, there are an estimated 8.7 million adults, making up about 4.4% of the population, who have ADHD[1]. Surprisingly, only around 2.6% of adults with adult ADHD were diagnosed during childhood[2].

Some additional demographics to shed some light: it does seem to impact those between 35 and 44 more (at 4.6%) and statistically, men bear the brunt more than women (5.4% vs 3.2%)[3].

Despite its perceived prevalence, it is estimated that about 20% of adults with ADHD are undiagnosed and of those who have received a diagnosis, only about 4% receive treatment[4].

Why is adult ADHD so underdiagnosed?

Ever wonder why adult ADHD often slips under the radar? Well, researchers point to a few things:

Lack of awareness and education[5]

One of the primary reasons why adult ADHD remains underdiagnosed is the lack of awareness and education surrounding the disorder. Most people still link ADHD with rowdy kids who can't sit still.

The misunderstanding leads many to overlook their symptoms and struggle in silence long into adulthood.

Stigma and misconceptions[6]

Stigmatization and misconceptions further complicate the diagnosis of adult ADHD. So many people believe that ADHD is just hyperactive kids or deliberate laziness and lack of discipline.

They write it off as a minor issue, or worse, not even real. These misconceptions can discourage individuals from seeking help or disclosing their struggles.

Difficulty accessing mental health services[7]

Even when individuals recognize their symptoms and seek a diagnosis, they may encounter difficulties accessing mental health services. Long wait times, limited availability of mental health professionals, and financial constraints can create barriers to diagnosis and treatment.

This problem is not unique to ADHD but is a broader issue within the healthcare system. It's unfortunate, but unavoidable.

Challenges in diagnosing ADHD in adults

Diagnosing ADHD in adults can be more challenging than in children. Symptoms can actually present differently in adults than they do in children.

In many cases, adults have developed coping mechanisms over the years, which may mask some of the disorder's symptoms. Not to be confused with ADHD masking which is the deliberate masking of symptoms in order to appear more neurotypical.

Coping mechanisms may be keeping multiple planners, setting alarms for everything, finding ways to fidget that aren't disruptive, writing everything down, etc.

Coping mechanisms are part of learning to live with ADHD, but when they've been perfected to the point they actually make it difficult to recognize symptoms, it can make it difficult to diagnose adult ADHD accurately.

Clinicians must consider two things:

1. A comprehensive medical and psychological history

2. The individual's current symptoms and their impact on daily life

These assessments can be time-consuming and may require specialized training, making it important to have knowledgeable healthcare professionals who can diagnose and treat adult ADHD. But, those specialists can be difficult to access.

Comorbidity of other mental health conditions such as depression[8] or substance abuse[1]

ADHD doesn't always roll solo. In fact, it often brings along friends. Adults with ADHD often experience other mental health conditions in addition to their primary diagnosis.

Conditions such as depression, anxiety, or substance abuse can be both a cause and a consequence of untreated ADHD.

About 20 to 25% of adults with ADHD also wrestle with anxiety[44] and those with ADHD are 50% more likely to develop a substance abuse problem[5].

Consequences of Flying Under the Radar

Unfortunately, undiagnosed and untreated ADHD can have a significant consequences:

- **Lower educational attainment and income:** Untreated ADHD can make school and work feel like climbing a mountain with no gear. Adults with untreated ADHD may struggle with academic and occupational challenges, which can lead to less schooling and reduced earning potential.

- **Poorer work performance and productivity:** ADHD's tag-along symptoms can make holding down a job a real challenge. ADHD symptoms, such as difficulty focusing, impulsivity, and disorganization, can hamper work performance and productivity, potentially leading to job instability or underemployment.

- **More marital problems and divorce:** You already know this if you're reading this book. Relationship difficulties are common for adults with untreated ADHD, which can strain marriages and lead to higher rates of divorce.

- **More difficulty in relationships.** It's not just romantic relationships, though. Issues with emotional regulation lead to frustration, impatience, and anger. The emotional reactivity can have an impact on interpersonal relationships—romantic, platonic, and professional.

- **Lower self-esteem and life satisfaction:** Living with undiagnosed ADHD can take a toll on how someone sees themself, leaving them feeling frustrated, overwhelmed, and isolated. Living with undiagnosed ADHD can erode self-esteem and overall life satisfaction.

I can wax poetic about the importance of early diagnosis and treatment, but everyone has different circumstances and this isn't always possible. Some don't have access to the medical professionals necessary. Some have developed such effective coping mechanisms, it completely masks identifying symptoms.

But diagnosis, when possible, can be helpful in the long run—not just for your relationship but for their own well-being.

Common Symptoms and Challenges

The tricky thing about ADHD? No two people present the same way. Symptoms vary from person to person. They can also change depending on the situation and the environment.

Stressful or overstimulating environments can exacerbate symptoms. But calming environments or activities the individual really enjoys can help calm them.

Even those with similar symptoms may present them differently. But if we're playing symptom bingo, the usual suspects include difficulty paying attention, impulsiveness, and restlessness[9][10][11].

In addition to these core symptoms, adults with ADHD may also have difficulties with executive functioning[9]. Executive functions are mental skills, or cognitive processes, that help you plan, prioritize, organize, monitor, and regulate your behavior. Think of it as the brain's backstage manager—it helps you plan, organize, and handle life's to-do list.

Executive Functions include:

WHAT IS ADULT ADHD?

Attention Control.

Function: The ability to regulate attention and focus, concentrate, and stay on task.

Impact: This is the stereotypical ADHD symptom. Individuals with ADHD can have difficulty focusing, getting easily distracted and often jumping from task to task without completion.

Working memory.

Function: the ability to hold and manipulate information in your mind.

Impact: If it feels like your partner is constantly forgetting things, this is why. Individuals with ADHD have trouble remembering and processing information, impacting tasks that require juggling multiple pieces of information simultaneously.

Inhibitory control.

Function: the ability to suppress inappropriate thoughts (often referred to as intrusive thoughts) or actions.

Impact: This is what causes the impulsivity associated with ADHD. It can look like actions taken without thought or considerations. Or, or can look like someone who blurts things out or interrupts when someone else is talking.

Cognitive flexibility.

Function: the ability to switch between different tasks or perspectives.

Impact: Individuals with ADHD can struggle with transitions. They may have trouble with changes in plans or procedures, which can often cause frustration.

- **Self-monitoring:** the ability to evaluate your own performance and adjust accordingly
- **Goal-directed behavior:** the ability to initiate, maintain, and complete tasks that are relevant to your goals
- **Planning and organization:** the ability to plan out tasks and organize thoughts.

Executive functioning difficulties can affect various domains of your life, such as:

- **Time management:** having trouble estimating how long tasks will take, meeting deadlines, or managing your schedule[6,10]
- **Organization:** having trouble keeping track of your belongings, paperwork, or finances as well as difficulty organizing thoughts[6,10]
- **Motivational regulation:** having trouble staying motivated, persistent, and initiating tasks.
- **Planning:** having trouble planning out tasks, prioritizing, and following through
- **Problem-solving:** having trouble identifying problems, generating solutions, or implementing strategies[10]

- **Self-regulation:** having trouble managing your emotions, motivation, stress level, or self-esteem[10]

Some other common symptoms of ADHD are:

- Problems focusing on a task[6][10]

- Trouble multitasking[6][10]

- Excessive activity or restlessness[6][10]

Types of ADHD

What most people don't know is there are actually multiple types of ADHD. The three main types are inattentive type, hyperactive-impulsive type, and combination type[12].

Predominantly Inattentive ADHD

Think of this as the focus wanderer. People with this type often find their minds taking unexpected detours. While you may deal with impulse control and hyperactivity on occasion, they are not the primary features of predominantly inattentive ADHD.

Inattention means having trouble focusing on tasks that require sustained mental effort, such as reading, writing, or listening. People with inattention may also have difficulty following instructions—written and verbal, remembering details, organizing their work, or switching between tasks. They may be easily distracted by external stimuli (such as noises or notifications) or internal thoughts (such as worries or fantasies). This type of ADHD is where the stereotypes tend to come in, the "squirrel!" concept.

You might see those with predominantly inattentive presentation[42]:

- Getting easily distracted by outside stimuli
- Making careless mistakes
- Appearing forgetful or "spacey"
- Procrastinating simple tasks
- Frequently losing things like their phone and keys

Predominantly Hyperactive-Impulsive ADHD

As the name states, individuals with this subtype of ADHD are impulsive and high energy. Inattentive moments might pop up, but they're usually playing second fiddle, overshadowed by the more pronounced symptoms of impulsivity and hyperactivity.

Hyperactivity means having excess energy or restlessness that makes it hard to sit still or relax. People with hyperactivity may feel the need to move around constantly, fidget with their hands or feet, talk excessively, or engage in risky behaviors. They may also experience boredom easily and seek stimulation or excitement on a whim.

Impulsivity means acting without thinking about the consequences or alternatives. People with impulsivity may have trouble controlling their impulses, such as blurting out comments, interrupting others, making rash decisions, or spending money recklessly. They may also struggle with delaying gratification, resisting temptations, or waiting for their turn.

Common indicators include[42]:

- An inability to remain seated

- A tendency to engage in constant verbal activity, often interrupting others

- A propensity for acting impulsively without taking potential consequences into account

- Difficulty with patience and waiting their turn

Combination ADHD

True to its name, this form of ADHD is a mix-and-match of symptoms drawn from both the inattentive and hyperactive-impulsive types. Those with combined-type ADHD may grapple with an array of symptoms, including challenges in maintaining focus, restlessness, impulsivity, and hyperactivity. Typically this diagnosis is made if the individual has at least six symptoms of each type.

Chapter Two

Myths & Misconceptions

If your partner—or even you—have ADHD, you may have encountered some myths and misconceptions about this condition. These are thrown around so often, we discussed them in the last chapter as a reason behind the underdiagnosis.

Here's the issue. It's one thing when the world throws around assumptions about ADHD and those who have it. But when you start brewing up your own batch of misconceptions about your partner, that's a whole different ball game. These false ideas? They're like the tiny cracks that can slowly mess with the foundation of your relationship—creating misunderstandings, hurt feelings, and even permanently damaging your relationship.

If your partner was diagnosed with diabetes or some other physical ailment out of their control, you would do everything you could to understand it and how you could help. You wouldn't blame them for things beyond their control.

So, why wouldn't it be the same for ADHD? It's not a choice your partner made—it's just a quirk in their brain wiring. Understanding that can be a game-changer in how you tackle the ups and downs together.

Myth #1: ADHD Isn't Real

One of the most pervasive myths about ADHD is that it is not a real disorder, but rather a convenient label for people who are lazy, irresponsible, or immature.

This myth is based on the assumption that people with ADHD can control their symptoms if they just try harder or use more willpower. Newsflash: not true! Not even close.

ADHD isn't some imaginary ailment. It is a recognized medical condition that affects the brain's ability to regulate attention, impulses, emotions, and executive functions. It is recognized by multiple major medical associations such as the National Institute of Health, the Centers for Disease Control and Prevention, and the American Psychiatric Association[13].

This isn't some made up mumbo jumbo. It's a neurodevelopmental disorder that genuinely impacts their everyday life.

Myth #2: People With ADHD Just Need To Try Harder

This one is worse than Myth #1 on many levels—the notion that folks with ADHD are just being lazy or need a motivational pep talk. This is so damaging, because this myth doesn't come quietly. It's spewed from the mouths of parents and partners.

People with ADHD are not lazy or unmotivated; they have a different brain wiring that makes it harder for them to focus, plan, organize, prioritize, and follow through on tasks.

Telling someone with ADHD to "focus" won't do them any good. It would be like asking someone who wears glasses to just see without them. Or telling someone with type 1 diabetes to just produce more insulin. That's not how it works.

Myth #3: Only Boys/Men Have ADHD

Men are more likely to have or develop adult ADHD than women, that's true. But, that doesn't mean women don't have it. 5.4% of men have ADHD vs 3.2% of women[3]. But, girls are actually more likely to be undiagnosed[13] or misdiagnosed[14].

Why? Because the symptoms present differently in men vs women.

Symptoms will still vary from person to person, but majoritively men tend to exhibit more hyperactive and impulsive symptoms causing them to be fidgety, disruptive, impulsive, impatient, and have mood swings[15,16].

Women, on the other hand, exhibit more inattentive symptoms making it difficult for them to focus, pay attention to details, stay organized, actively listen, and impacts their memory[15].

Since women have less obvious symptoms that can be more easily covered up with coping mechanisms, their symptoms are often overlooked.

Myth #4: People With ADHD Can't Focus—Ever

Those with ADHD do often struggle with focus—it is called **attention** *deficit* hyperactivity disorder. But, that doesn't mean they can't focus at all. In fact, many with ADHD also have periods of hyperfocus[15].

Hyperfocus is a common symptom that involves intense and prolonged concentration on a task, activity, or topic[17]—or even a person. It can sometimes be a coping mechanism for those with ADHD when dealing with distraction and boredom[18].

Like a lack of focus, hyperactivity can have negative consequences. Your partner may neglect other important tasks or relationships, lose track of time, or become irritable when interrupted[17,19].

Myth #5: Only Children Have ADHD

For those who believe ADHD is a real condition, many believe that it only affects children, that it is something they will outgrow as they age. Hyperactivity and impulsivity tend to decrease with age, but that doesn't mean ADHD has suddenly disappeared. In fact, about 60% of those with ADHD have symptoms that persist into adulthood[43].

Many adults with ADHD still struggle with inattention, distractibility, procrastination, forgetfulness, and other challenges that affect their personal and professional lives. Some adults may not even realize that they have ADHD until later in life, when they face increased demands and responsibilities that expose their difficulties.

Myth #6: ADHD Is The Same For Everyone

Many believe that ADHD is a one-size-fits-all disorder. It is easily diagnosed and treated and anyone who is hyperactive must have ADHD. Right? Wrong.

ADHD is a complex and heterogeneous condition with diverse presentations, underlying causes, and comorbidities. That was a mouthful. Essentially, it means that it can vary widely from person to person, and even within the same person over time. It's not always easy to spot and diagnose. And one person's symptoms may not match another's.

There are three main types of ADHD that present different symptoms, different co-occurring conditions (such as anxiety, depression, or learning disabilities), and different responses to medication and other interventions.

There is no single test or treatment. Each person with ADHD needs a comprehensive and individualized assessment and a tailored and holistic approach to manage their symptoms and optimize their strengths.

Recognizing the Realities of ADHD

The struggles those with ADHD face are not due to a lack of intelligence, talent, or potential. People with ADHD have many strengths and abilities that can help them succeed in life. Some of these strengths include:

- Creativity, originality, and innovation

- Curiosity, enthusiasm, and passion

- Flexibility, adaptability, and resilience

- Energy, dynamism, and spontaneity

- Empathy, compassion, and generosity

- Humor, wit, and charm

These strengths are not always recognized or appreciated by others, especially in a society that values conformity, productivity, and efficiency. People with ADHD often face discrimination from others and may also face rejection from those in their professional and personal lives due to the symptoms they deal with.

Because of this, it is very common for those with ADHD to internalize negative messages and develop low self-esteem, guilt, shame, and self-doubt. For something they can't control.

Your partner's journey with ADHD may involve overcoming various challenges, but in your relationship, you have the opportunity to be a pillar of support and understanding. Instead of reinforcing societal stigmas, your role is to celebrate and appreciate the unique strengths that come with ADHD.

Acknowledge the creativity, innovation, and out-of-the-box thinking that your partner brings into your life. Recognize the moments of hyperfocus, where their intense concentration leads to incredible insights and accomplishments. Be a source of encouragement, helping them navigate a world that may not always understand or appreciate their exceptional qualities.

In your relationship, strive to create an environment where your partner feels accepted, valued, and loved for who they are, ADHD and all.

Reducing the Stigma

Don't let your relationship suffer simply because you don't fully understand everything your partner is going through. Reduce the stigma and increase the acceptance.

Here are some suggestions:

- **Educate yourself and others about ADHD.** Learn the facts and share them with your partner, family, friends, co-workers, and anyone else who may benefit from knowing more about this condition. Use reliable sources of information, such as books, websites, podcasts, or experts. Avoid misinformation, stereotypes, or myths that may perpetuate stigma or misunderstanding. Luckily, you're already on your way thanks to this book!

- **Seek professional help.** If your partner has ADHD, or you suspect they may have it, encourage them to seek professional help. A qualified mental health professional can help with the diagnosis, treatment, and support of ADHD. They can also help with any other issues that may be affecting mental health, such as anxiety, depression, or trauma. Professional help can make a big difference in quality of life and your relationship. But, remember this is a personal choice and they may not be interested.

- **Join a support group.** Make sure your partner knows they are not alone in their journey. But, know that you are not alone either. There are many people who share your experiences, challenges, and hopes. Joining a support group can help you connect with others who understand what you are going through, and who can offer you advice, encouragement, and friendship. You can find support groups online or in your local community, or you can start your own.

- **Advocate for them and encourage them to advocate for themself and others.** They have the right to be treated with respect, dignity, and fairness. They have the right to access the resources and accommodations that they need to thrive in their personal and professional life. They have the right to express their opinions, needs, and preferences. They have the right to be themself. Advocate for them and others who have ADHD, and challenge any discrimination or injustice that you encounter. You can also join or support organizations that promote the rights and interests of people with ADHD.

- **Celebrate their strengths and achievements.** You have many reasons to be proud of your partner. They have overcome so many obstacles and accomplished many goals. They have contributed to their family, their work, their community, and society. They have made a positive difference in the world. Even if the world doesn't always see it that way. Celebrate and acknowledge your partner's strengths and achievements. Appreciate the uniqueness and diversity of each other, and of all people with ADHD.

Chapter Three

The Impact on Relationships

ADHD can have a significant impact on your relationships, both positive and negative. On the one hand, ADHD can bring excitement, creativity, spontaneity, and passion to your relationship. On the other hand, ADHD can also create challenges, conflicts, misunderstandings, and frustrations.

It can be so easy to focus on the negative only.

ADHD can create some unique difficulties in relationships that range from irritating to relationship-ending. ADDitude conducted a survey of married individuals with ADHD and found that 38% reported that their marriage had teetered close to divorce in the past. Another 22% said divorce had "crossed their mind[8]."

Another ADDitude study found that 42% reported that ADHD impacted their sex life "a lot" while 51% said that it put a damper on their intimacy with their partner[20].

Divorce rates where at least one partner has ADHD are nearly twice as high as those who are not impacted by it[21]. Those statistics are concerning, but they don't mean your relationship is doomed.

Understanding your partner's ADHD and how it can impact your relationship is a step in the right direction.

Individuals with ADHD often experience social difficulties, social rejection, and interpersonal relationship problems as a result of their inattention, impulsivity, and hyperactivity[22].

Those who are easily distracted may not appear to be listening closely to loved ones, while those with time-management challenges may be frequently late—or may even forget social plans and errands altogether[22]. Impulsive symptoms can lead to risky financial decisions or other reckless behavior that can cause tension with others, particularly in romantic relationships.

Despite the challenges associated with ADHD in relationships, understanding and empathy can pave the way for growth and resilience. It's crucial to recognize that ADHD brings a spectrum of experiences—both enriching and demanding—to your partnership. Yes, it may be easy to focus on the negative, but don't forget to see the whole picture.

While divorce rates may be higher in relationships where at least one partner has ADHD, it's essential to remember that statistics don't determine the outcome of any specific relationship. What matters most is the commitment to understanding, supporting, and navigating the unique dynamics introduced by ADHD.

It won't be easy by any means, but what relationship is? It's a journey that requires patience, compassion, and a willingness to learn and adapt together.

ADHD and Communication

Communication is undeniably the cornerstone of any flourishing relationship, serving as the bridge that connects individuals on emotional, intellectual, and interpersonal levels. The importance of communication makes the challenge of communication for those with ADHD more notably pronounced.

Communication is particularly difficult when at least one partner has ADHD. They're either not listening, or they are... but they don't retain a thing you said. You may find that you repeat yourself constantly.

Maybe your partner is like mine with a tendency to start conversations in the middle like you've been living in their head with them. Luckily for me, we've been at this a while and I get him so I'm usually a happy little caboose on his train of thought.

The characteristic inattention of individuals with ADHD may manifest as difficulty focusing on conversations, leading to a potential mismatch between spoken words and the recipient's comprehension. This can result in misunderstandings, missed cues, and an overall sense of disconnection.

Impulsivity, another hallmark of ADHD, introduces an additional layer of complexity to interpersonal communication. Quick, unplanned reactions may lead to misunderstandings or unintended hurt feelings. They may speak over you because they can't stop the thought from coming out. The impulsive nature of their responses may even keep them from fully listening and comprehending what you're saying.

Hyperactivity, though often associated with physical restlessness, can also manifest in verbal communication. Rapid speech or an eagerness to interrupt may be unintentional manifestations of hyperactivity, making it challenging for individuals with ADHD to engage in measured and reciprocal dialogue.

Some of the communication problems that people with ADHD may experience include[23]:

- Difficulty listening and paying attention to what their partner is saying

- Difficulty expressing their thoughts and feelings clearly and coherently

- Difficulty staying on topic and following the conversation

- Difficulty taking turns, leading to them interrupting their partner

- Difficulty reading and responding to their partner's verbal and non-verbal cues

- Difficulty giving and receiving feedback and criticism

These communication problems can lead to misunderstandings, arguments, resentment, and disconnection in your relationship. Due to the reality of their diagnosis, your partner may struggle to get past this issue on their own—or even be aware that it is a problem.

Navigating communication challenges in a relationship impacted by ADHD requires a collaborative and empathetic approach. Understanding the specific communication difficulties associated with ADHD is the first step toward fostering effective and meaningful interaction.

It might feel like this is all on you, but it's not. It might just take your initiative and an empathetic approach for your partner to recognize the problem and start working with you toward some kind of solution.

There are strategies that can enhance communication within relationships involving individuals with ADHD. They won't fix everything. These are more like bandaids but they can foster growth that leads to better habits long-term.

To improve your communication, you and your partner can try the following strategies:

Active Listening Strategies:

Implement active listening techniques, such as repeating back what your partner has said to ensure understanding. Encourage your partner to express themselves in a manner that works for them, whether through written communication or other creative outlets.

The key here is to find what works for you both. Don't make them feel like a child while you slowly repeat everything the other person says.

Structured Communication:

Introduce structured communication methods, like setting aside designated times for important discussions or using visual aids to stay on topic. Creating a communication-friendly environment can help mitigate distractions and enhance focus. It might seem strange to schedule a conversation, but it might help the ADHD partner better prepare their thoughts and take a more active role in the conversation.

Some ways to implement this:

- Choose a good time and place to talk, when you are both calm and focused

- Use eye contact, body language, and gestures to show your interest and attention

- Use active listening skills, such as paraphrasing, summarizing, and asking questions

- Use "I" statements, such as "I feel", "I need", or "I want", to express your feelings and needs

- Use positive and constructive language, such as "I appreciate", "I agree", or "I suggest", to give feedback and suggestions

- Use humor, compliments, and appreciation to lighten the mood and show your affection

- Use a timer, a signal, or a code word to remind yourself to take turns and avoid interruptions

- Use a notebook, a recorder, or a smartphone to write down or record important points or agreements

- If the issue is larger, consider using a mediator, a counselor, or a coach to help you resolve conflicts or improve your communication skills

Patience and Flexibility:

Cultivate patience and flexibility in your communication style. Recognize that your partner may need extra time to process information or organize their thoughts. Be open to adapting your communication methods to accommodate their unique needs. And, don't show your irritation and impatience; it will only make it harder for them to communicate.

Understand that your partner may have different communication styles and preferences than you. Respect your partner's pace and rhythm. Allow your partner to finish their thoughts and sentences and adapt your communication to the situation and the context[24].

Establishing Clear Communication Patterns:

Work together to establish clear communication patterns. This includes setting expectations for turn-taking, finding non-intrusive ways to signal when interruptions occur, and creating a safe space for expressing thoughts and feelings without fear of judgment.

Some ideas for regulating the conversation:

- **Be clear and concise.** Use simple and direct language. Avoid ambiguity or vagueness. State your main point first, and then provide details or examples. Repeat or summarize the key points at the end of the conversation[24].

- **Be specific and concrete.** Use facts and evidence to support your statements. Avoid generalizations or assumptions. Give examples or scenarios to illustrate your points. Use numbers or dates to quantify your information[24].

- **Be respectful and empathetic.** Use a polite and friendly tone. Avoid sarcasm or criticism. Acknowledge your partner's feelings and perspectives. Validate your partner's experiences and emotions. Express your appreciation and gratitude for your partner[24].

- **Be attentive and responsive.** Pay attention to your partner's verbal and nonverbal cues. Maintain eye contact and appropriate body language. Show interest and curiosity in what your partner is saying. Ask questions and provide feedback. Avoid distractions or interruptions[24].

- **Be honest and trustworthy**. Tell the truth and keep your promises. Share your thoughts and feelings openly and sincerely. Avoid hiding or withholding information. Admit your mistakes and apologize when necessary. Build trust and confidence with your partner[24].

Non-Verbal Cues and Feedback:

Recognize the significance of non-verbal cues in communication. Encourage your partner to use cues that signal their level of engagement or comprehension. Similarly, be attuned to their cues and respond with understanding and patience.

Feedback and Criticism:

Approach feedback and criticism with sensitivity. Frame discussions around growth and improvement rather than focusing solely on perceived shortcomings. Establish a supportive environment where both partners feel comfortable expressing concerns and working collaboratively toward solutions.

Sometimes it can be something simple. My partner really does start conversations in the middle. Often. And while I can usually follow his train of thought without much help, sometimes that's not possible—like when we live nine hours away from each other at separate colleges. Instead of getting angry or frustrated with him, I developed an easy solution. I would just say "context" and he would give me more information.

Professional Support:

Consider seeking professional support, such as couples therapy or counseling, to navigate communication challenges. A trained therapist can provide guidance, teach effective communication strategies, and facilitate a deeper understanding between partners.

Emotional Regulation and Impulsivity

People with ADHD often have difficulty regulating their emotions, due to their impaired executive functions and their heightened sensitivity to stimuli. They may experience intense and frequent mood swings, such as anger, sadness, anxiety, or excitement. They may also act on their impulses, without thinking of the consequences, such as saying hurtful things, spending money, or sometimes even cheating on their partner.

Now, that's not to say that all will be forgiven simply because it's a result of their ADHD.

While understanding the impact of ADHD on emotional regulation is crucial, it's equally important to acknowledge the boundaries within a relationship. While ADHD can offer insights into certain behaviors, it doesn't excuse actions that breach trust or inflict significant harm, such as cheating.

What can you do after a breach of trust?

Setting Clear Boundaries:

Establish clear and respectful boundaries within your relationship. Communicate openly about behaviors that are unacceptable, regardless of the influence of ADHD. This might include discussing the emotional fallout from impulsive actions and determining the line between the effects of ADHD and actions that breach trust.

Addressing Consequences:

Recognize that, even with the challenges of ADHD, there are consequences for actions. While it's essential to approach your partner's struggles with empathy, it's equally vital to address the impact of certain behaviors on the relationship. Seek professional guidance if necessary to navigate complex issues.

Maintaining Personal Well-Being:

Prioritize your own well-being. Understand that forgiveness and moving forward may not be possible in every situation. If certain actions, such as cheating or excessive spending, have caused irreparable damage, it's essential to prioritize your emotional health and make decisions that align with your values and boundaries.

Seeking Professional Guidance:

In situations where trust has been broken, consider seeking professional guidance. Couples therapy or counseling can provide a structured space to address the emotional fallout, work through the complexities, and determine whether rebuilding trust is a viable path for both partners.

Open Communication:

Maintain open and honest communication about your feelings and concerns. Expressing the impact of specific actions on your emotional well-being allows for a more transparent and constructive conversation about the future of the relationship.

Remember, every relationship is unique, and the decision to move forward after a breach of trust is deeply personal. While ADHD provides context for certain behaviors, it doesn't negate the importance of accountability and the need for mutual respect within the relationship. Balancing understanding with a commitment to your own boundaries is key to navigating the complexities that may arise.

Helping your partner with their emotional regulation and impulsivity

Your partner may not be able to regulate their emotions or control their impulses on their own. Seeking professional help can go a long way for many, but you'll need to be proactive too.

Open Communication about Emotions:

Encourage open communication about emotions. Create a safe space where your partner feels comfortable expressing their feelings without judgment. Validate their emotions and work together to identify healthy ways to cope with intense moods.

Joint Strategies for Emotional Regulation:

Collaborate on strategies for emotional regulation. This could involve identifying triggers, establishing calming routines, or practicing mindfulness techniques together. Finding shared activities that promote emotional well-being can be a bonding experience.

Recognizing Impulsive Behaviors:

Be attentive to impulsive behaviors that may arise during emotional highs or lows. If your partner struggles with impulsivity, establish a system for gently redirecting them or creating a pause before acting on urges. This may involve a predetermined signal or phrase to signal the need for a moment of reflection.

Encouraging Professional Support:

Acknowledge that regulating emotions and managing impulsivity can be challenging, and seeking professional help is a constructive step. A mental health professional can offer guidance, coping strategies, and a structured approach to addressing these aspects of ADHD. Support from therapy or counseling can benefit both individuals and the relationship.

Learning Together:

Educate yourselves together about ADHD and its impact on emotional regulation. Understanding the neurological underpinnings of ADHD can foster empathy and diminish misconceptions.

Establishing Boundaries:

Work together to establish healthy boundaries. Open discussions about behaviors that may result from impulsive actions and collaborate on setting boundaries that ensure both partners feel respected and secure in the relationship.

Reinforcing Positive Coping Mechanisms:

Celebrate small victories when your partner successfully navigates challenging emotional moments or resists impulsive actions. Positive reinforcement can encourage the development of healthier habits.

Remember, your role is not to control or change your partner but to provide support and understanding. By approaching emotional regulation and impulse management as a team, you can foster an environment that promotes growth, self-awareness, and emotional well-being within your relationship.

Strategies for managing emotions and impulses as someone with ADHD

These strategies are for the partner with ADHD, but supporting them throughout the process can make all the difference. It is important to understand, though, that their inability to overcome these symptoms does not mean you have failed or that they don't want to put in the effort. Remember that their ADHD is not something they can control.

To manage emotions and impulses, you and your partner can try the following strategies:

- Identify and label your emotions, such as "I am feeling angry", "I am feeling anxious", or "I am feeling happy"

- Understand and accept your emotions, without judging or suppressing them

- Express and release your emotions, in healthy and appropriate ways, such as talking, writing, crying, or exercising

- Seek and offer support, from your partner, your friends, your family, or a professional

- Practice relaxation techniques, such as breathing, meditation, yoga, or massage

- Practice mindfulness, by paying attention to the present moment, without dwelling on the past or worrying about the future

- Practice cognitive-behavioral techniques, by challenging and changing your negative thoughts and beliefs

- Practice self-care, by eating well, sleeping well, exercising, and having fun

- Use medication, therapy, or coaching, if needed, to help you control your symptoms and improve your functioning

- Use coping skills, such as counting to ten, walking away, or distracting yourself, to prevent or stop impulsive actions

- Use rewards and consequences, such as praise, incentives, or penalties, to motivate or discourage impulsive behaviors

- Use reminders and cues, such as notes, alarms, or calendars, to help you remember your goals and commitments

Intimacy and Connection

Intimacy and connection are the foundation of any healthy and satisfying relationship. However, intimacy and connection can be challenging for people with ADHD.

Some of the intimacy and connection problems that people with ADHD may experience include:

- Difficulty showing interest and attention to their partner

- Difficulty expressing affection and appreciation to their partner

- Difficulty initiating and maintaining physical and sexual contact with their partner

- Difficulty sharing and listening to their partner's thoughts and feelings

- Difficulty spending quality time and doing activities with their partner

- Difficulty being consistent and reliable in their relationship

Navigating intimacy and connection in a relationship affected by ADHD requires a thoughtful approach that considers the unique challenges associated with inattention, hyperactivity, and impulsivity.

These intimacy and connection problems can lead to dissatisfaction, loneliness, boredom, and even resentment in your relationship. These difficulties can be made even more frustrating if your initial courtship was the exact opposite.

Hyperfocus Courtship

You'll remember from Chapter 2 that hyperfocus is a phenomenon where individuals with ADHD become intensely absorbed in a task, activity, topic—or person.

One of the paradoxes of ADHD and relationships is that people with ADHD can sometimes exhibit hyperfocus in the early stages of a relationship, when they are intensely attracted to and interested in their partner.

It can make a partner seem very attentive, passionate, and romantic. They may shower their partner with attention, affection, and gifts, and make them feel like the center of their world, also known as "love bombing[25]."

However, hyperfocus courtship can also have some drawbacks. Namely, that it isn't likely to last. While hyperfocus might have played a significant role in the initial courtship, it's essential to acknowledge that maintaining such intense focus over time can be challenging.

The hyperfocus courtship creates unrealistic expectations that are inevitably thrashed as that initial excitement fades and the intense focus wanes.

The end of the hyperfocus courtship does not mean your partner has lost interest in you, but it may feel that way. Especially if their ADHD symptoms make them seem even less attentive.

Fostering Intimacy and Connection

So, what can you do to help establish and foster intimacy and connection when ADHD symptoms cause a divide?

Open Dialogue About Needs:

Foster open communication about the intimacy and connection needs of both partners. Encourage your partner to express their feelings and challenges, and share your own. Collaborate on finding strategies that work for both of you, ensuring that each person's needs and desires are considered.

Create a Routine:

Establishing routines can be beneficial for individuals with ADHD. Whether it's dedicated quality time, regular check-ins, or planned activities, a consistent routine provides structure and predictability, contributing to a more stable and satisfying connection.

Explore Non-Traditional Intimacy:

Recognize that intimacy extends beyond traditional expressions. Explore non-traditional ways to connect emotionally, such as writing letters, creating shared projects, or engaging in activities that align with both partners' interests. This can be a valuable way to foster connection in a manner that accommodates ADHD-related challenges.

Adapt to Changing Dynamics:

Understand that relationships naturally evolve over time. Be flexible and adaptive in your expectations, recognizing that the dynamics you experienced during the initial courtship may shift. Hyperfocus can be an inevitability for those with ADHD, but it is impossible to maintain long term. Embrace the growth and change within your relationship, finding new ways to connect and sustain intimacy when that initial hyperfocus comes to an end.

By acknowledging the specific intimacy and connection challenges associated with ADHD and actively working together, you can build a foundation of understanding, patience, and creativity. Embracing the nuances of your relationship and adapting to changing dynamics allows for a more resilient and satisfying connection over the long term.

The Inevitability of Anger

Anger is a normal and natural emotion that can indicate that something is wrong or needs to change. However, anger can also be harmful and destructive, if it is not managed properly.

This is a double edged sword because it is not just your partner's emotional regulation you need to deal with—it's your own anger at the situation.

Anger in the ADHD Partner

The ADHD partner may experience anger due to their emotional regulation issues, which are caused by the imbalance of neurotransmitters in their brain. They may have trouble controlling their anger, expressing it appropriately, or calming down after an angry episode.

Anger may manifest in different ways for individuals with ADHD. This can include inappropriate or aggressive expressions such as yelling, swearing, or physical actions. They may also suppress their anger, or turn it inward, which can lead to depression, anxiety, or self-harm. Understanding the range of manifestations is crucial in approaching the issue empathetically.

Again, I want to reiterate that all is not forgiven simply because it was caused by their ADHD. But understanding the root cause can start you on the path to understanding and helping your ADHD partner manage their symptoms appropriately.

Recognize that anger may be a symptom of deeper issues. It can be a response to frustration, overwhelm, stress, or feelings of inadequacy.

They may feel angry for various reasons, such as:

- Feeling frustrated, overwhelmed, or stressed by their daily challenges

- Feeling misunderstood, criticized, or rejected by their partner or others

- Feeling ashamed, guilty, or insecure about their ADHD symptoms or their performance

- Feeling bored, restless, or dissatisfied with their current situation

- Feeling impulsive, reactive, or defensive in response to a trigger or a provocation

This has always been particularly difficult in my relationship. My partner doesn't express his anger loudly, but it comes on quickly and he is often unwilling to communicate when he is in this state of mind. It can be frustrating for me because it often feels like the anger and frustration he is feeling is directed at me, when that is almost never the case.

Setting expectations and explaining my side of things helped in this situation. Now instead of telling me he's not upset, he gives me a reason—even if that reason is "I don't know." It has made a world of difference for us.

My personal experience highlights the importance of setting expectations and explaining your perspective. Establishing a communication routine can help your partner express their feelings and provide reassurance.

It can also be helpful to work together to try and identify the root cause and identify triggers. Understanding the root cause allows for proactive measures to avoid or manage these triggers. This collaborative approach empowers both partners to navigate situations that may lead to anger more effectively.

Encourage open dialogue about the specific triggers and stressors that contribute to anger, fostering an environment where your partner feels comfortable expressing their emotions. Encourage them to express their emotions and reassure them that you are there to listen without judgment.

The Non-ADHD Partner

The non-ADHD partner may experience anger due to the situation, which is caused by the mismatch of expectations and realities in their relationship. They may have trouble coping with their anger, communicating it effectively, or resolving it constructively.

They may also have trouble empathizing with their partner, or accepting their partner's ADHD as a valid explanation for their behavior.

Do you find yourself feeling:

- Hurt, betrayed, or disappointed by your partner's actions or inactions

- Resentful, burdened, or exhausted by your partner's demands or needs

- Neglected, ignored, or unappreciated by your partner

- Frustrated, confused, or hopeless about your partner's symptoms or their treatment

- Powerless, helpless, or hopeless about your relationship or your future together

Your anger is valid. Your feelings matter, and it's okay to express them. But blaming your partner for aspects beyond their control is not productive nor is it valid.

It is important to manage anger in a healthy and productive way, by:

Recognizing Signs and Triggers:

Identifying personal signs and triggers of anger allows for proactive management and prevention. This awareness is crucial for both partners to foster a supportive environment. Don't just focus on your ADHD partner's signs and triggers, recognize and acknowledge your own as well.

Taking Time-Outs and Breaks:

When anger arises, taking a time-out or a break provides an opportunity to cool down and regain composure. It prevents escalating tensions and allows for more rational communication. Adding a bit of structure to these time-outs can help you to communicate more effectively when you return to the conversation.

Practicing Relaxation Techniques:

Engaging in relaxation techniques, such as breathing exercises, meditation, or physical activity, contributes to emotional well-being and aids in anger management.

Seeking Professional Help:

Professional support, whether through therapy, medication, or coaching, can provide tools and strategies for effectively managing anger within the context of ADHD-related challenges.

Expressing Anger Respectfully:

Expressing anger assertively, using "I" statements and active listening, fosters a more constructive dialogue between partners. This approach encourages understanding and empathy.

Apologizing and Forgiving:

Apologizing and forgiving when necessary contribute to a healthier emotional environment. Acknowledging mistakes and granting forgiveness are integral to rebuilding trust and connection.

Finding Positive and Constructive Coping Mechanisms:

Embracing positive and constructive coping mechanisms, such as problem-solving, compromise, or humor, strengthens the resilience of the relationship.

Anger is an inherent aspect of any relationship, particularly when ADHD is a factor. By learning how to deal with anger in a healthy and productive way, both partners can overcome challenges and cultivate a relationship that thrives on mutual understanding and support.

Chapter Four

Empathy and Compassion

Some of the key foundational skills for a partner of someone with ADHD are empathy, patience, and compassion. These qualities serve as pillars to foster understanding, resilience, and mutual support.

Empathy is the ability to understand and share the feelings of another person. It is instrumental in forging a strong connection with your partner. Empathy allows you to stand beside your partner, offer support, and minimize conflicts.

And, patience is a virtue...one many of us forget to practice. It's not just a virtue, though, it's a vital component in the complex puzzle of adult ADHD relationships.

While easier said than done, exercising patience is crucial in moments of frustration, misunderstanding, or during the learning curve of managing ADHD-related challenges.

Putting these skills into practice requires ongoing effort and commitment. Even with the techniques outlined in this chapter, there will be both good days and bad days, great days and days where you just want to give up.

Try to change your perspective.

Acknowledging imperfections—both in oneself and in the relationship—is essential. Embrace the understanding that perfection is not the goal, but rather a continuous effort toward improvement.

No one is perfect. No relationship is perfect. But, taking these steps and making this effort can significantly benefit your relationship.

Developing Empathy for Your Partner with ADHD

Empathy is a powerful force that helps maintain social order and cooperation. It is the mechanism that allows people to understand and relate to others. Empathy is a necessary precursor to intimacy, trust, and belonging.

But, empathy is not something that you either have or don't have. It is a skill that you can learn and improve over time. Which means, it is something you can choose to work on for the sake of your relationship.

Here are some techniques that can help you to develop empathy for your partner with ADHD:

Listen actively

You will see this mentioned several times throughout the book. In fact, it's already been mentioned a few times. Hint: it's pretty important.

Active listening is a skill that can help you communicate better with someone. It means paying attention to what the other person is saying, showing interest and empathy, and asking questions to deepen your understanding.

When your partner is talking to you, pay attention to what they are saying, how they are saying it, and what they are not saying. Don't interrupt, judge, or offer solutions unless they ask for them. Just listen and try to understand their perspective.

Now, this can be incredibly difficult for someone with ADHD so it may feel like the effort is all one sided. But this isn't something you have to practice on your own. Both you and your partner can work on actively listening.

For someone with ADHD, you can try:

- **Slowing down.** If you talk too fast, you may miss important details or overwhelm your listener. Try to pause between sentences and take a breath before continuing[26].

- **Waiting your turn.** If you interrupt or jump in while someone is talking, you may make them feel frustrated or ignored. Wait until they finish their sentence before you respond or ask a question. But be careful. Don't simply wait for your turn to speak without making the effort to listen to what your partner is saying. If you're worried you'll lose the thought, write it down.

- **Seeing what you hear.** Try to visualize the story or message that the other person is trying to convey. Pretend that you will be quizzed on it later and that you have to explain it clearly[26].

- **Asking open-ended questions.** Instead of asking yes or no questions that can end the conversation quickly, ask questions that invite the other person to share more about their thoughts, feelings, and experiences[27,28].

- **Validating their emotions.** When the other person expresses an emotion, acknowledge it and show that you care. Don't dismiss, minimize, or criticize their feelings[27].

For the non-ADHD partner:

- **Put yourself in their shoes.** Try to imagine what it is like to be in your partner's situation. Think about how their ADHD affects them in different aspects of their life, such as work, school, relationships, health, etc. Think about how they might feel about their challenges and how they cope with them.

- **Be curious.** Show genuine interest in learning more about your partner's ADHD and how it impacts them. Your partner may be hyperfixating on something. And, yes, they may drop it in a few days, but they are interested in it now. Don't dismiss it simply because it may be a fleeting interest.

Practicing Patience

Patience is another essential skill for a partner of someone with ADHD—or really just for a partner of...anyone. Patience means being able to tolerate delays, difficulties, mistakes, or changes without getting angry or frustrated. It can help you to avoid conflicts and maintain a positive relationship with your partner.

Here are some tips for practicing patience:

Cope with moments of frustration. When you feel frustrated by your partner's behavior or actions related to their ADHD, take a deep breath and calm yourself down before reacting. Remind yourself that this is not personal and that it doesn't mean that they don't love you or appreciate you.

Understand that much of this is out of their control. Your partner's ADHD is not something that they chose or can easily change by themselves. It is a neurodevelopmental condition that affects how they think, feel, and act in different situations. They may have difficulties with attention span, impulsivity, organization, planning, memory, etc., but these are not intentional or malicious.

When I started my research and began to develop an understanding of what my partner was going through, it changed my perspective. Understanding what he could and could not control really helped me to regulate my own reactions. I was more patient, more empathetic, and more willing to work with him to develop the strategies and coping mechanisms to help our relationship thrive. A decade later, we still have our difficulties but we're also still thriving thanks in large part to my willingness to understand and empathize.

Focus on the positive aspects. Instead of dwelling on the negative consequences of your partner's ADHD on your relationship or life goals, focus on the positive aspects of having them as your partner. Think of their:

- Creativity
- Enthusiasm
- Generosity
- Loyalty, etc.

Try to appreciate the little things that they do for you instead of worrying about the things they don't—or can't because of how their ADHD impacts them.

My partner is not a planner. He doesn't always think before he acts and sometimes that can be hurtful. But he's incredibly supportive of everything I do even when it's something that doesn't interest him. He actively shares the household responsibilities—particularly ones that I don't enjoy (like the dishes *shiver*).

I still get frustrated. His ADHD can still cause issues in our relationship. But I've learned to focus on the positives more than the negatives and to work together to deal with the symptoms when they create problems in our relationship.

I'm not perfect by any means and it's not a stretch to assume that you aren't either. If your partner is willing to work with your flaws and focus on the positive, then you can be too.

Building a Supportive Environment

EMPATHY AND COMPASSION

A supportive environment is one where both you and your partner feel safe, understood, and valued[29]. By building empathy and practicing patience, you're already working your way toward this.

A supportive environment helps you and your partner to thrive and grow as individuals and as a couple. Here are some ways to build a supportive environment:

Create a safe and understanding atmosphere. Make sure that both of you feel comfortable sharing anything with each other without fear of judgment, criticism, or rejection.

- Create rules and boundaries that respect each other's needs and preferences, and enforce them consistently.

- Don't make promises that you can't keep or set expectations that are unrealistic.

- Be honest, respectful, and compassionate with each other.

Understand what they can and cannot control. Your partner may have some things under their control, such as their attitude, behavior, or effort, and some things out of their control, such as their symptoms, medication side effects, or external factors.

Don't blame them for things that are beyond their control or make them feel guilty for things that are within their control. Instead, try to help them to identify what they can do to improve themselves or cope better, and what they need to accept or let go of.

I know with my partner, some of the things that would drive me crazy were things he wasn't even aware he was doing (or not doing). Making him aware of them allowed him to address the issues. And, maybe I had to repeat myself a few times—maybe a hundred or so on occasion—but it helped us to keep moving forward.

Recognizing the distinction between what your partner can and cannot control is paramount. Whether it's managing their attitude, behavior, or external circumstances, understanding these dynamics fosters empathy.

Refrain from assigning blame for factors beyond their control, and instead, work collaboratively to identify constructive ways to cope and improve.

Build a stronger relationship. Celebrate the small victories and milestones, and be supportive during setbacks. Encourage individual pursuits and personal growth.

A supportive environment extends beyond the relationship itself. Foster an atmosphere where both partners can pursue their interests, goals, and personal well-being. This not only enriches individual lives but also contributes positively to the relationship.

Honesty, respect, and compassion should be the pillars of your interactions. This foundation of trust allows both partners to navigate challenges with a shared understanding.

Stay consistent. Consistency is vital in upholding a supportive atmosphere. Establish clear rules and boundaries that acknowledge each other's needs and preferences. Strive to enforce these guidelines consistently, creating a sense of stability and reliability in your relationship.

Remember that building a supportive environment is an ongoing process. Be open to learning from each other and adapting to the changing needs of both individuals. By prioritizing understanding, communication, and mutual growth, you lay the foundation for a resilient and nurturing partnership.

Chapter Five

Strategies for Effective Communication

Effective communication serves as the cornerstone for understanding and connection in any relationship. It involves not only expressing your thoughts and feelings but also actively listening to your partner's perspective.

Building on this foundation, cultivating healthy communication habits can significantly enhance the strength of your relationship.

By prioritizing and nurturing effective communication, you strengthen the bonds of understanding and connection in your relationship, fostering an environment where both partners can feel supported, valued, and emotionally connected.

But, to understand how to effectively communicate with your ADHD partner, you need to understand how they struggle in terms of communication.

Communication Difficulties Caused By Adult ADHD

Those with ADHD struggle more with communication due to their executive function challenges.

Challenges with executive function can impact someone's ability to plan, organize, and execute their thoughts and words, which are the foundation of communication.

Someone with ADHD may deal with communication difficulties like:

Talking too much or too little. People with adult ADHD may have difficulty finding the right balance between sharing and listening in a conversation. They may talk too much and interrupt others, or they may talk too little and miss important information or cues. They may also switch topics abruptly or go off on tangents without finishing their main points[30]. Or they may start a conversation in the middle as though you've been following their mental gymnastics right alongside them—something my partner is often guilty of.

Forgetfulness or spacing out. People with adult ADHD may have trouble remembering what they were going to say or what others said during a conversation. They may forget names, dates, details, or instructions. They may also lose track of the context or the flow of the conversation and get confused or distracted[30]. About 80% of children with ADHD struggle with working memory, a problem that persists into adulthood[31]. So, you may need to repeat yourself twenty or so times. Remember, they're not trying to be difficult. They genuinely do not remember what you said and it isn't because they weren't listening.

This was (and is) often the source of the most frustration in my relationship. My partner has a habit of asking me a question I (quite literally) answered less than five minutes prior. It is a work in progress, but he is conscious of the issue and makes the effort to listen more actively so that he can better retain the information I'm relaying.

Finding the right words or choosing inappropriate words. People with adult ADHD may struggle to express themselves clearly and accurately in words. They may use filler words, slang, jargon, or vague terms that are not understood by others—or maybe they insert random obscure movie quotes into conversation like my partner and his brother. They may also say things that are inappropriate, offensive, or insensitive for the situation[30,32].

These communication issues can cause misunderstandings, conflicts, frustration, and embarrassment for people with adult ADHD and their partners, friends, coworkers, and family members.

However, there are some strategies that can help improve communication skills for people with adult ADHD. Some of these strategies are:

- **Taking notes or recording conversations.** This can help people with adult ADHD remember what was said and avoid forgetting important information[30].

- **Asking questions or paraphrasing what was said.** This can help people with adult ADHD check their understand-

STRATEGIES FOR EFFECTIVE COMMUNICATION 59

ing and show interest in the conversation[30].

- **Using a call and response style of communication.** One of the active listening strategies people use is repeating back what someone has said to ask for clarification or show that you understand. This was particularly effective for my partner and I.

- **Using simple and direct language** that avoids ambiguity or confusion[30]. This not only helps others understand what you're saying, it can help you better organize your thoughts.

- **Organizing thoughts before speaking** and using transitions to guide the listener through the message[30]. This will help you to stay on task too.

- **Using a positive and assertive tone** that shows confidence and respect[30].

- **Being aware of how much you're interrupting others** and apologizing if necessary[30].

- **Acknowledging that the other person is speaking.** Even when what they've said doesn't require a response. They need to know you heard them.

Developing Strategies for Effective Communication

Now that you better understand where your partner is struggling, you can work together to build strategies for more effective communication. From active listening to navigating non-verbal cues, these tools foster a deeper understanding, navigate challenges, and strengthen bonds.

Active Listening

We have already covered the first step toward effective communication in the previous section. And, I can pretty much guarantee you'll see it again. Another hint: it's *super* important.

Active listening is about more than simply fostering empathy, it is an important part of deliberate communication.

This is a crucial skill that involves fully focusing on, understanding, and responding to the person you are speaking to. It builds rapport, trust, and, of course, empathy.

Key techniques for active listening include maintaining eye contact, avoiding distractions, asking clarifying questions, and providing both verbal and non-verbal feedback[33][34].

Clear and Structured Communication

Isn't this the same thing as effective communication? Yes and no. It is a major ingredient of the complete recipe, but it is still only one piece. Clear and structured communication is a strategy that allows you to convey your message in a way that is easy to follow and comprehend.

This is excellent for communicating with someone who has ADHD and struggles to stay focused and process information. But it is also an excellent way for those with ADHD to structure their communication so that others can easily understand them.

It can help avoid confusion, ambiguity, and errors. It involves using concise language, organizing information logically, and being mindful of non-verbal cues. Active listening complements clear communication by ensuring that messages are accurately received[34].

How can you communicate in a clear and structured way? We've gone over active listening, think of this as "active" communicating:

- **Use concrete language.** Employing specific and straightforward language reduces ambiguity. Instead of vague or abstract terms, opt for words that precisely convey the intended message. This helps individuals with ADHD grasp information more easily.

- **Break information into chunks.** Breaking down complex information into smaller, manageable chunks makes it more digestible. Providing information in a step-by-step manner allows for better comprehension and retention, catering to the potential challenges in processing lengthy or intricate details.

- **Avoid ambiguity.** Ambiguous statements or unclear instructions can lead to confusion. Strive for clarity by being explicit and avoiding double meanings. When expectations are clear, it reduces the likelihood of misunderstandings.

- **Establish communication rituals.** Consistent communication rituals create predictability and structure. This can include setting specific times for important conversations, using designated spaces for discussions, or developing routines for checking in with each other. Predictability is especially beneficial for individuals with ADHD.

- **Encourage active participation.** Foster engagement by encouraging questions, seeking feedback, and ensuring that both parties actively participate in the communication process. This involvement reinforces understanding and reduces the chances of information being overlooked.

- **Clarify expectations.** Clearly communicate expectations regarding roles, responsibilities, and shared commitments. Having a shared understanding of expectations promotes a sense of order and minimizes the potential for misunderstandings or unmet expectations.

- **Use visuals if necessary.** Visual representation complements verbal communication, offering additional support for individuals who may benefit from multiple modes of information processing.

Conflict Resolution Techniques

No matter how much effort you put in, no matter how patient or empathetic you are, conflict is inevitable. Conflict resolution techniques can help navigate disagreements and maintain healthy relationships.

In relationships where one or both partners have ADHD, communication difficulties can amplify conflicts making it even more crucial to have effective strategies.

Some strategies for resolving disagreements constructively are:

Identifying the root cause of the conflict. Instead of placing blame or pointing fingers, individuals express their feelings and concerns from a personal perspective. This approach fosters open communication, as it avoids putting the other person on the defensive and encourages empathy and understanding.

Acknowledging each other's feelings and perspectives. Acknowledgment is a powerful tool in conflict resolution. Both partners should feel heard and validated in their emotions and perspectives. Encourage individuals to express empathy and understanding toward each other, acknowledging the validity of their feelings even if they don't fully agree. This creates a foundation of mutual respect and fosters an environment where both individuals feel safe sharing their thoughts and emotions.

Focusing on the issue, not the person. In the heat of a conflict, it's easy to direct frustration or blame at the other person. Emphasize the importance of focusing on the specific issue at hand rather than making personal attacks. This is where "I" statements come in.

Using "I" statements to express your needs and concerns. Instead of placing blame or pointing fingers, individuals express their feelings and concerns from a personal perspective. This approach fosters open communication, as it avoids putting the other person on the defensive and encourages empathy and understanding.

Listening actively and respectfully to each other. In conflict situations, active listening takes on heightened importance. Ensure that both partners are not only expressing their viewpoints but also actively listening to each other. This involves paraphrasing and reflecting back the partner's concerns, demonstrating a genuine effort to understand and validate their perspective. Active listening not only promotes empathy but also lays the groundwork for a more collaborative resolution.

Agreeing on a plan of action and follow up. Resolution isn't just about finding common ground; it's also about implementing a plan to prevent similar conflicts in the future. Collaboratively develop a plan of action that addresses the root cause and incorporates compromises from both sides. Establish clear expectations, responsibilities, and timelines. Following up on the agreed-upon plan ensures accountability and provides an opportunity to reassess and make adjustments if needed. Regular check-ins create a proactive approach to conflict prevention and resolution.

Chapter Six

Setting Realistic Expectations

Managing Expectations in the Relationship

Living with a partner with ADHD brings its own set of challenges, but finding a delicate balance between expectations and reality is crucial for a thriving relationship. It's essential to recognize that your partner's brain operates differently, and embracing this uniqueness is the first step towards building a strong foundation.

Managing expectations involves establishing boundaries, setting goals, and learning more about each other—and how your partner's ADHD affects them. By defining your personal duties and expectations, you can create a structured relationship-life balance and foster positive, trusting relationships with your partner.

Embracing Differences

Your partner's ADHD may manifest in various ways, impacting communication, organization, and focus. Accepting these differences is key to fostering understanding. Remember that ADHD is not a choice; it's a neurological condition that influences behavior and perception. By acknowledging these differences, you pave the way for open and compassionate communication.

Open Dialogue

Establishing a channel for open communication is vital. Regularly check in with each other about expectations and how they align with reality. This creates a space for both of you to voice concerns, share feelings, and work together to find solutions. Be patient and listen actively, as understanding each other's perspectives is a cornerstone of a successful relationship.

Balancing Responsibilities

In any partnership, a fair distribution of tasks and responsibilities is fundamental. When ADHD is in the picture, it becomes even more crucial to find a balance that accommodates your partner's unique strengths and challenges.

It involves distributing tasks and obligations equitably, considering each other's strengths and limitations, and communicating openly about expectations.

Identify Strengths and Challenges

Work together to identify your partner's strengths and challenges. This self-awareness is empowering and allows for a more strategic delegation of responsibilities. By acknowledging areas where your partner excels, you can assign tasks that align with their strengths, making the division of labor more efficient and satisfying for both.

Collaborative Planning

Sit down and collaboratively plan your daily and long-term responsibilities. Discuss and decide on roles based on each other's preferences and capabilities. Flexibility is key; some days may require adjustments, and being adaptable ensures a smoother navigation of your shared responsibilities.

Goal Setting and Accomplishments

Celebrating both small victories and setting achievable goals is a powerful tool in maintaining a positive and supportive environment.

Setting goals together can help you align your aspirations and work towards shared objectives. Celebrating accomplishments along the way can strengthen your bond and motivate both partners to continue growing together[35].

Celebrate Small Wins

ADHD can sometimes make even the smallest tasks challenging. Celebrate these victories, no matter how minor they may seem. Acknowledge the effort your partner puts into everyday activities and express genuine appreciation. Small affirmations go a long way in boosting morale and fostering a sense of accomplishment.

Set Achievable Goals

When setting goals, be realistic and break them down into manageable steps. This approach makes larger tasks less overwhelming and provides a roadmap for success. Encourage your partner to set their own goals, ensuring they are attainable and align with their strengths.

Chapter Seven

Seeking Professional Help

Living in a relationship affected by adult ADHD can be challenging, and at times, seeking professional help becomes a valuable resource.

There are two sides to seeking professional help: help for your relationship and help for your ADHD partner. First, I'd like to discuss the importance of diagnosis. You may remember from chapter 1, that it is estimated that about 20% of adults with ADHD are undiagnosed and of those who have received a diagnosis, only about 4% receive treatment[4].

The Importance of Diagnosis

If you think you or your partner might have ADHD, it is important to seek professional help. Getting a proper diagnosis can help you understand yourself better and access appropriate treatment options. A diagnosis can also help you explain your difficulties to others and request accommodations if needed.

You may also remember that it can be difficult to diagnose ADHD in adults due to the developed coping mechanisms and other factors. Healthcare professionals use the Diagnostic and Statistical Manual of Mental Disorders (DSM-5)—the "official" handbook for mental health professionals.

According to DSM-5 critetia[36], an individual must meet the following conditions to be diagnosed with ADHD:

- You must have at least five symptoms of inattention **and/or** five symptoms of hyperactivity-impulsivity that are present for at least six months and cause significant impairment in two or more settings (such as home, work, school, or social situations)

- Some of these symptoms must have been present before the age of 12

- These symptoms cannot be better explained by another mental disorder (such as anxiety, depression, bipolar disorder, or schizophrenia) or by a medical condition (such as thyroid disorder, sleep apnea, or substance abuse)

To determine whether or not you meet these criteria, a mental health professional will conduct a comprehensive assessment that includes:

- **A clinical interview**: asking you about your current symptoms, childhood history, family background, medical history, and other relevant factors

- **Behavioral observation**: observing how you behave in different situations and settings

- **Psychological testing**: administering standardized tests or questionnaires to measure your attention span, memory capacity, executive functioning skills, and other cognitive abilities

- **Collateral information**: obtaining information from other sources who know you well (such as family members, partners, friends, or coworkers) to corroborate your self-report

If it is determined that you have adult ADHD, then your doctor will likely diagnose you with one of the three subtypes: inattentive, hyperactive-impulsive, combination.

The subtype of ADHD can change over time, depending on the severity and frequency of your symptoms. The subtype can also influence the type of treatment that is best suited for you.

Getting a proper diagnosis can help you understand your condition better and access appropriate treatment options.

Therapy and Counseling Options

Therapy can be an effective way to better understand, accept, and manage the effects of ADHD both on the individual and on the relationship. It can also help with other mental health conditions, such as depression and anxiety, that often come with ADHD.

For your ADHD partner, if they're willing, there are some types of therapy that can help them manage ADHD symptoms. These include[37]:

- **Behavioral Therapy:** Focused on changing specific behaviors and developing coping strategies.

- **Psychoeducation:** Provides information and tools to better understand and manage ADHD.

- **Coaching:** Offers personalized support and guidance in setting and achieving goals.

- **Skills Training:** Equips individuals with practical skills to address challenges associated with ADHD.

If you're struggling to navigate the complexities of a relationship impacted by Adult ADHD, there are therapy options for you to pursue as a couple. These include:

- **Cognitive-Behavioral Therapy (CBT):** CBT is a goal-oriented therapeutic approach that focuses on identifying and changing negative thought patterns and behaviors. It can be particularly effective for partners seeking practical strategies to manage the challenges associated with ADHD. CBT can empower both individuals to develop coping mechanisms and enhance communication skills.

- **Couples Therapy:** Couples therapy provides a safe space for partners to explore their feelings, improve communication, and work collaboratively towards strengthening their relationship. A skilled therapist can help both partners understand the impact of ADHD on their relationship dynamics and provide guidance on building a more resilient connection.

Medication and Treatment

Medication can be an important part of managing ADHD symptoms. It can help with all types of ADHD and their main symptoms: impulsivity, inattention, and hyperactivity. However, research has found that medication alone may not address every symptom of ADHD. And there are many who are not willing to deal with the side effects, some of which can be just as debilitating as the symptoms they're treating.

I know for my partner the side effects were cumbersome and he felt they were a hindrance to our relationship when we first started dating. He was tired and irritable by the end of the day and he didn't want to take that out on me. So, he made the choice to stop taking the medication.

But, later in college, we made the choice together for him to try a different medication. He was struggling with some of his classwork at the time and needed something more than his coping mechanisms could manage. He's not on any medications now and there are many things we still struggle with, but he is one of those with ADHD who can manage without.

There are many, who need the medication just to function at a normal level. The decision to take medication or go without will be up to each individual and their doctors.

In some cases, though, medication may be a valuable component of managing ADHD symptoms. There are two types of ADHD medication:

- **Stimulant Medications.** Stimulant medications, such as methylphenidate and amphetamine-based drugs, are commonly prescribed to manage ADHD symptoms. These medications can enhance focus and attention. However, they may not be suitable for everyone, and their effectiveness can vary.

- **Non-Stimulant Medications.** Non-stimulant medications, like atomoxetine and guanfacine, offer alternative options with fewer side effects than stimulant medications. These medications may be recommended based on individual needs and medical considerations.

As with any medication, your partner should speak with a medical professional and do the research to determine if the suggested treatment will be the right choice for them.

A Holistic Approach

Now, I know that buzzwords like holistic tend to turn people off. But, holistic medicine is often misunderstood. Holistic medicine is about treating the whole person, not just the symptoms. It is about finding physical, mental, emotional, social, and spiritual well-being.

It is often a mix of conventional medicine and alternative methods. A holistic approach to treating ADHD could include medication, nutrition, lifestyle changes, therapy, and coaching[37].

Since medication alone is not always a solution, and since many choose to go without, a holistic approach to ADHD treatment is crucial. Your partner and their doctors can come up with the right mix of treatment for them.

The Role of Support Groups

There are support groups for nearly everything out there. So it is no surprise there are support groups and communities for individuals suffering from ADHD. Given the nature of ADHD and the impact it can have on relationships, there are also support groups available for partners.

Support groups provide a valuable space for partners to share experiences, gain insights, and receive emotional support from others who understand the unique challenges of living with someone with ADHD.

Some support groups out there include:

- **CHADD** (Children and Adults with Attention-Deficit/Hyperactivity Disorder) is an ADHD organization that offers both in-person and online support communities[38]. They even have an annual conference. You can visit their website (https://chadd.org/) or contact CHADD by phone at 301-306-7070.

- **ADDA** (The Attention Deficit Disorder Association) has many resources for people with ADHD, including workshops, support groups, and a peer-mentor program[39]. You can visit their website (https://add.org/).

- **ADHD Marriage** offers support groups specifically for non-ADHD partners of individuals with ADHD. These groups are done over Zoom[40]. You can learn more on their website (https://www.adhdmarriage.com/).

You can also contact the National Resource Center (NRC)/ADHD Helpline Health Information Specialists at 866-200-8098, Monday-Friday, 1 p.m. – 5 p.m. EST.

These are just a few examples of the support groups available. There may be other local or online support groups that cater to the needs of people with ADHD and their partners. It's always a good idea to explore different options and find a group that suits your specific requirements.

Living with a partner with ADHD can be emotionally taxing. Support groups provide a safe space to express feelings, receive encouragement, and gain perspective on navigating the ups and downs of the relationship.

Seeking professional help is a proactive and constructive step in managing the complexities of a relationship affected by adult ADHD. Whether through therapy, medication, or joining support groups, these resources can provide valuable tools and insights to strengthen your connection and enhance the well-being of both partners. Remember, reaching out for support is a sign of strength and commitment to the health of your relationship.

Chapter Eight

Self Care for Partners

Living in a relationship affected by adult ADHD can be both rewarding and challenging. As a partner, it's crucial to prioritize your own well-being to navigate the complexities.

Self-care is a fundamental aspect of maintaining overall well-being and is particularly crucial for your physical health, mental health, and mental well-being. It can help your relationships and your emotional well-being as well as prevent burnout, increase productivity and creativity, and enhance your self esteem. It even has long-term health benefits.

There's really no downside here.

In this chapter, we'll discuss taking care of your mental health, finding balance in your relationship, and avoiding burnout.

Taking Care of Your Mental Health

It can be easy as a partner to someone with ADHD to worry about their partner's mental health first. And, if you have kids, you end up becoming an afterthought. But you really shouldn't.

Taking care of your mental health could look like joining support groups as discussed in the last chapter or seeking professional help for yourself. Or, it might simply look like healthy habits like eating well, exercising regularly, or getting enough sleep.

Prioritize "Me" Time

Allocate regular time for activities you enjoy. Whether it's reading, exercising, or simply relaxing, having moments for yourself is vital.

Establish Boundaries

Clearly communicate your needs and set boundaries. This helps create a balance between supporting your partner and preserving your own energy.

Seek Support

Connect with friends, family, or support groups. Sharing your experiences and feelings with others who understand can provide emotional support.

Practice Stress-Relief Techniques

Incorporate stress-relief techniques into your routine, such as deep breathing, meditation, or mindfulness. These practices can help manage the inevitable stress that may arise.

Finding Balance in the Relationship

Striving for balance is essential to ensure that both partners' needs are met. But it is about more than that. Maintaining a sense of self is crucial for a healthy relationship and a healthy you. By finding a healthy equilibrium, you can create a supportive environment that benefits both you and your partner[41].

You can preserve your identity and build a stronger relationship by:

Pursuing Personal Interests

Engage in activities that are meaningful to you, whether it's a hobby, sport, or creative pursuit. This contributes to your overall fulfillment.

Setting Individual Goals

Establish personal goals and aspirations. This not only helps you grow but also reinforces your sense of identity outside of the relationship.

Communicating Your Needs

Openly communicate your need for independence and personal space. A healthy relationship involves mutual understanding and respect for each other's individuality.

Planning Quality Time Together

Set aside intentional quality time with your partner. This ensures that the relationship remains a source of joy and connection rather than solely a space for managing challenges.

Avoiding Burnout

We've all heard about a work-life balance, but having a relationship-life balance is equally important—regardless of whether or not your partner has ADHD. But the demands of supporting a partner with ADHD can be overwhelming, making it even more important to pay attention to your mental health and avoid burnout.

Burnout is a state of physical, emotional, and mental exhaustion resulting from prolonged exposure to high levels of stress. There are physical and emotional symptoms of burnout and it can be very difficult to recover.

Be on the lookout for signs of burnout:

Emotional Exhaustion

Individuals experiencing burnout often feel emotionally drained and depleted. They may find it challenging to cope with the demands of their responsibilities, leading to a sense of helplessness and fatigue.

Reduced Professional Efficacy

In a work context, burnout is often accompanied by a decrease in professional efficacy. Individuals may experience a decline in their ability to meet job demands, resulting in feelings of incompetence and a negative impact on job performance.

Cynicism and Detachment

Burnout can manifest as a growing sense of cynicism or detachment. Individuals may become emotionally distant, disengaged, and develop a pessimistic outlook, especially towards their work or caregiving roles.

Physical Symptoms

Burnout is not limited to emotional and mental aspects; it can also have physical manifestations. Physical symptoms may include headaches, gastrointestinal issues, sleep disturbances, and increased susceptibility to illnesses.

Reduced Personal Accomplishment

Individuals experiencing burnout may perceive a decreased sense of personal accomplishment. They may feel that their efforts go unrecognized, leading to a diminished sense of achievement and satisfaction in their work or responsibilities.

Neglect of Self-Care

Burnout often results in the neglect of self-care activities. Individuals may struggle to find the time or motivation to engage in activities that promote well-being, further exacerbating the cycle of exhaustion and detachment.

Impaired Cognitive Function

Prolonged stress and burnout can impact cognitive functions such as memory, concentration, and decision-making. Individuals may find it challenging to focus on tasks, leading to decreased efficiency and effectiveness.

Interpersonal Challenges

Burnout can strain interpersonal relationships, both at work and in personal life. Cynicism and emotional distance may affect communication and collaboration, leading to difficulties in maintaining healthy connections.

Burnout can occur in any area of life where there is chronic stress and an imbalance between demands and resources. Addressing burnout typically involves a combination of self-care, setting boundaries, seeking support, and, in some cases, making changes to the work or caregiving environment.

Recognizing the signs of burnout early on is crucial. But implementing effective strategies to prevent yourself from reaching it is even more important. How can you avoid burnout? By prioritizing your mental health and finding balance.

Chapter Nine

Strengthening the Bond

You're here because you want to help your relationship thrive. And, now that you have a better understanding of your partner's ADHD and how it impacts your relationship, you're well on your way.

But building a resilient and fulfilling relationship involves intentional efforts to strengthen the emotional connection and rediscover joy together. Reading this book is only step one.

I've given you strategies for communication, self-care, and seeking support. All of which can help your relationship. But now it's time to discuss strengthening your bond.

Nurturing Emotional Intimacy

If you think of a relationship as a tapestry, you can think of emotional intimacy as the vibrant thread that weaves partners together on a profound level. That connection is the heartbeat of a resilient and fulfilling relationship.

So how can you nurture emotional intimacy? You may not be surprised to find that we've already covered several of the ways you can build a stronger relationship:

Practice Active Listening

Yup! Here it is again. Engage in active listening during conversations. Make a conscious effort to understand your partner's perspective and validate their feelings.

Communicate Openly

It's not just about communicating effectively, you need to communicate openly. Accept each other and what the other person says without judgment. Practice honesty and understanding.

Exercise Empathy

It's not just about listening and communicating, you need to connect emotionally. Being there for them emotionally can build and strengthen your emotional connection with your partner.

Share Your Stories

Set aside time to share personal stories and experiences. This builds a deeper understanding of each other's lives, fostering emotional intimacy.

Express Gratitude

Regularly express gratitude for each other. This simple practice can strengthen the bond by acknowledging and appreciating the positive aspects of your relationship.

Create a Shared Vision

Discuss and create a shared vision for the future. This can include both short-term and long-term goals, fostering a sense of unity and collaboration.

Activities and Strategies to Connect

Building upon the foundation of emotional closeness, is connection. Weave new memories, foster a sense of unity and togetherness, and remember why you fell in love in the first place.

Explore New Hobbies

Discover new activities or hobbies together. Whether it's cooking classes, hiking, or art projects, shared experiences can deepen your connection.

Plan Regular Date Nights

Prioritize regular date nights to spend quality time together. This dedicated time fosters a sense of intimacy and provides an opportunity to reconnect.

Engage in Playful Activities

Embrace playfulness in your relationship. Engage in activities that bring out joy and laughter, such as board games, playful competitions, or outdoor adventures.

Travel Together

Plan occasional getaways or travel experiences. Exploring new places together can create lasting memories and strengthen your bond.

Rediscovering Joy Together

Don't just strengthen your relationship, rediscover joy. You can create emotional intimacy, connect, share happiness by engaging in fun and meaningful activities and rediscovering joy together.

Surprise Each Other

Plan surprises to keep the relationship exciting. This could be as simple as a thoughtful note, a surprise dinner, or an unexpected gesture.

Celebrate Milestones

Take time to celebrate both big and small milestones in your relationship. Reflecting on shared achievements reinforces the positive aspects of your journey together.

Attend Workshops or Classes

Explore workshops or classes together. This could include relationship-building seminars, dance classes, or anything that piques your mutual interest.

Practice Mindfulness Together

Incorporate mindfulness practices into your routine. Whether it's meditation, yoga, or nature walks, these activities can create a sense of calm and connection.

Remember, the effort you invest will contribute to the growth and vitality of your relationship.

Chapter Ten

The Road Ahead

You're standing at the intersection of your past relationship and your future relationship with your partner. It's time to reflect on the progress made, acknowledge the milestones achieved, and set your sights on the road ahead.

In this final chapter, we explore the importance of celebrating progress, the continuous journey of learning and adaptation, and sustaining a loving relationship built on understanding and resilience.

Celebrating Progress

Acknowledge Growth

Take a moment to reflect on the growth and progress both as individuals and as a couple. Celebrate the challenges overcome and the lessons learned.

Recognize Milestones

Identify and celebrate the milestones achieved in your relationship. Whether they are big or small, each accomplishment contributes to the strength of your bond.

Express Gratitude

Express gratitude for the journey you've shared. Acknowledge the efforts invested by both partners, fostering a sense of appreciation for the resilience and commitment shown.

Continuing to Learn and Adapt

Cultivate a Learning Mindset

Approach the future with a learning mindset. Recognize that growth is a continuous process, and each experience presents an opportunity to learn more about yourselves and each other.

Communicate Openly

Maintain open communication about your needs, challenges, and aspirations. A transparent and honest dialogue lays the foundation for ongoing understanding and adaptation.

Seek Professional Support When Needed

Don't hesitate to seek professional support if challenges arise. Whether through therapy, counseling, or support groups, professional guidance can provide valuable insights and strategies.

Sustaining a Loving Relationship

Prioritize Connection

Make intentional efforts to prioritize emotional and physical connection. Regularly check in with each other, fostering an environment where both partners feel seen and heard.

Nurture Individual Well-being

Continue to prioritize self-care and individual well-being. A strong, loving relationship is built on the foundation of two fulfilled individuals.

Adapt Relationship Strategies

Be willing to adapt your relationship strategies as needed. Recognize that flexibility is key in navigating the evolving dynamics of a relationship impacted by Adult ADHD.

Foster Mutual Support

Cultivate a sense of mutual support. Encourage each other's goals and dreams, providing a source of strength and encouragement.

The road ahead is a continuation of the shared journey, a path where the commitment to understanding, adapting, and loving each other deepens with every step. As you celebrate progress, embrace ongoing growth, and sustain the love you've nurtured, remember that the strength of your relationship lies not just in overcoming challenges but in the unwavering commitment to face the future together.

May your road ahead be filled with shared joys, continued learning, and the enduring warmth of a loving partnership.

Chapter Eleven

Embracing Love and Growth

Love requires care, understanding, and continuous nourishment to thrive. Every journey is unique, but every journey will be marked by its unique challenges and triumphs. A thriving relationship is a testament to the strength of your commitment and the depth of your connection.

In embracing love and growth, we acknowledge that every relationship is a living, breathing entity—an evolving dance between two individuals. Celebrating the progress made and milestones achieved serves as a compass, guiding you forward. Each challenge overcome, each lesson learned, and every shared moment of joy contributes to the rich tapestry of your shared history.

As you continue on the road ahead, recognize that growth is not only a personal journey but a collective one, where the bond between partners is strengthened through continuous learning and the shared experiences that shape your narrative.

May your relationship be a source of joy, a haven of support, and a canvas for the expression of love in all its forms. May it be a testament to the beauty of love's journey—a journey enriched by the shared experiences, the lessons learned, and the unwavering commitment to the growth and well-being of both partners.

Wishing you a future filled with love, understanding, and the boundless possibilities that come from embracing both the challenges and joys that life and love bring.

Sam

Chapter Twelve

References

1. ADHD Statistics And Facts In 2023 | Forbes Health. https://www.forbes.com/health/mind/adhd-statistics/

2. People over 50 with ADHD 'overlooked' for diagnosis and treatment, say experts | Medical Express. https://medicalxpress.com/news/2023-09-people-adhd-overlooked-diagnosis-treatment.html

3. ADHD Statistics: How Common Is It? | Mind Diagnostics. https://www.mind-diagnostics.org/blog/adhd/adhd-statistics-how-common-is-it

4. Calls to address overlooked ADHD in adults aged 50 and over | New Atlas. https://newatlas.com/medical/adhd-older-adults/

5. Untreated ADHD in Adults: Signs, Causes, Impact, and Treatment | Verywell Mind. https://www.verywellmind.com/untreated-adhd-in-adults-signs-causes-impact-and-treatment-5222929

6. ADHD symptoms are underdiagnosed in adults | Mayo Clinic Press. https://mcpress.mayoclinic.org/mental-health/adult-adhd-and-how-to-treat-it/

7. An ADHD diagnosis in adulthood comes with challenges and benefits | APA. https://www.apa.org/monitor/2023/03/adult-adhd-diagnosis

8. Data and Statistics About ADHD | CDC. https://www.cdc.gov/ncbddd/adhd/data.html

9. What is Adult attention deficit hyperactive disorder and its possible symptoms, causes, risk and prevention methods? | MSN. https://www.msn.com/en-us/health/condition/Adult-attention-deficit-hyperactive-disorder/hp-Adult-attention-deficit-hyperactive-disorder?source=conditioncdx

10. Adult attention-deficit/hyperactivity disorder (ADHD) | Mayo Clinic https://www.mayoclinic.org/diseases-conditions/adult-adhd/symptoms-causes/syc-20350878

11. Adult ADHD: Symptoms, diagnosis, and treatment | Medical News Today. https://www.medicalnewstoday.com/articles/adult-adhd

12. 3 Types of ADHD: Hyperactive, Inattentive, and Combined | ADDitude. https://www.additudemag.com/3-types-of-adhd/

13. 8 common myths about ADHD | Understood. https://www.understood.org/en/articles/common-myths-about-adhd

14. ADHD in Women vs. Men: Does Gender Play a Role in Symptoms? | Psych Central. https://psychcentral.com/adhd/adhd-and-gender

15. ADHD in Women: Signs and Symptoms | Verywell Mind. https://www.verywellmind.com/add-symptoms-in-women-20394

16. Female vs Male ADHD | The ADHD Centre. https://www.adhdcentre.co.uk/female-vs-male-adhd/

17. Understanding Hyperfocus and ADHD | Cleveland Clinic. https://health.clevelandclinic.org/hyperfocus-and-adhd/

18. Hyperfocus and the ADHD Brain: Intense Fixation with ADD | ADDitude. https://www.additudemag.com/understanding-adhd-hyperfocus/

19. What Is Hyperfocus and How Does It Affect Kids and Adults? | Healthline. https://www.healthline.com/health/adhd/adhd-symptoms-hyperfocus

20. ADHD Marriage: Statistics, Trends, and Personal Stories | ADDitude. https://www.additudemag.com/adhd-marriage-statistics-personal-stories/

21. Can Your Relationship Survive ADHD? | US News Health. https://health.usnews.com/health-news/family-health/brain-and-behavior/articles/2010/09/28/can-your-relationship-survive-adhd

22. ADHD and Relationships | Psychology Today. https://www.psychologytoday.com/us/basics/adhd/a

dhd-and-relationships

23. The Effects of ADHD on Communication | ADD Resource Center. https://www.addrc.org/effects-adhd-communication/

24. How ADHD Can Affect Adult Communication | Apheleia Speech. https://apheleia-speech.com/adhd-adult-communication/

25. Love Bombing and ADHD: Hyperfocus? Thrill Seeking … | ADDitude. https://www.additudemag.com/love-bombing-adhd-hyperfocus/

26. Improve Listening Skills with Adult ADHD | ADDitude. https://www.additudemag.com/listening-skills-better-listener-adult-adhd-tips/

27. ADHD Listening Problems: Focus and Attention | ADDitude. https://www.additudemag.com/adhd-listening-problems/

28. Listen Up! Listening When You Have ADHD - ADHD Coach | My Attention Coach. http://myattentioncoach.com/adhd/listen-up-listening-when-you-have-adhd/

29. 5 Tips to Be More Empathetic in Your Relationship | Psych Central. https://psychcentral.com/relationships/how-to-be-more-empathetic-in-relationship

30. "I Didn't Mean It!" How ADHD Affects Communication | ADDitude. https://www.additudemag.com/webinar/how-to-communicate-better-adhd-strategies/

31. ADHD and Memory: Effects, Tips, Treatment & More | Healthline. https://www.healthline.com/health/adhd/adhd-memory

32. The Effects of ADHD on Communication | ADD Resource Center. https://www.addrc.org/effects-adhd-communication/

33. Effective Communication | HelpGuide.org. https://www.helpguide.org/articles/relationships-communication/effective-communication.htm

34. Use active listening skills to effectively deal with conflict | MSU. https://www.canr.msu.edu/news/use_active_listening_skills_to_effectively_deal_with_conflict

35. Managing Expectations (So They Don't Manage You) | Science of People. https://www.scienceofpeople.com/managing-expectations/

36. Adult attention-deficit/hyperactivity disorder (ADHD) | Mayo Clinic.

https://www.mayoclinic.org/diseases-conditions/adult-adhd/symptoms-causes/syc-20350878

1. ADHD Treatment: Therapy, Medication, and More | Psych Central. https://psychcentral.com/adhd/treatment-for-attention-deficit-hyperactivity-disorder-adhd

2. How to Find an ADHD Support Group | Verywell Mind. https://www.verywellmind.com/how-to-find-an-adhd-support-group-5324827

3. Support Groups for Adults | Attention Deficit Disorder Association. https://add.org/adhd-support-groups/

4. Non-ADHD Partner Support Groups | ADHD and Marriage. https://www.adhdmarriage.com/page/non-adhd-partner-support-groups-melissa-orlov

5. How to Be Supportive of Your Partner with Mental Illness | NAMI. https://www.nami.org/Blogs/NAMI-Blog/November-2018/How-to-Be-Supportive-of-Your-Partner-with-Mental-I

6. Symptoms of Attention-Deficit Hyperactivity Disorder (ADHD) | Verwell Mind.https://www.verywellmind.com/adhd-symptoms-4157281

7. Our Current Understanding of Adult ADHD | NCBIhttps://www.ncbi.nlm.nih.gov/pmc/articles/PMC4301030/

8. Adult ADHD (Attention Deficit Hyperactive Disorder) | ADAA.https://adaa.org/understanding-anxiety/related-illnesses/other-related-conditions/adult-adhd

About the Author

Sam is a seasoned copywriter and editor with expertise in the health and wellness field and a unique perspective on adult ADHD relationships. While she may not hold a medical degree, her expertise lies in the realm of real-life experience.

Married to a wonderful man who happens to have ADHD, Sam brings an authentic understanding of the challenges and joys that come with navigating relationships in the context of ADHD.

When she's not writing, she's wrangling her husband, a daughter, three dogs, and a cat. Yep, it's a bit of a circus, but it keeps things interesting!

Printed in Great Britain
by Amazon